A day in the life of
Harold the doctor

Monica Hughes

Heinemann
LIBRARY

www.heinemann.co.uk/library
Visit our website to find out more information about **Heinemann Library** books.

To order:
☎ Phone 44 (0) 1865 888066
▤ Send a fax to 44 (0) 1865 314091
▦ Visit the Heinemann Bookshop at www.heinemann.co.uk/library to browse our catalogue and order online.

First published in Great Britain by Heinemann Library, Halley Court, Jordan Hill, Oxford OX2 8EJ, part of Harcourt Education.
Heinemann is a registered trademark of Harcourt Education Ltd.

Editorial: Jilly Attwood and Claire Throp
Design: Jo Hinton-Malivoire and bigtop, Bicester, UK
Models made by: Jo Brooker
Picture Research: Catherine Bevan
Production: Lorraine Warner

Originated by Dot Gradations
Printed and bound in China by South China Printing Company

ISBN 0 431 16521 1 (hardback)
06 05 04 03 02
10 9 8 7 6 5 4 3 2 1

ISBN 0 431 16526 2 (paperback)
06 05 04 03 02
10 9 8 7 6 5 4 3 2 1

British Library Cataloguing in Publication Data
Hughes, Monica
    A day in the life of a doctor
    610.6'952
A full catalogue record for this book is available from the British Library.

Acknowledgements
The publishers would like to thank the following for permission to reproduce photographs:
All photos by Tudor Photography.

Cover photograph reproduced with permission of Tudor Photography.

Special thanks to Dr Harold Hin and all the staff at Hightown Surgery, Banbury.

The publishers would like to thank Annie Davy for her assistance in the preparation of this book.

Every effort has been made to contact copyright holders of any material reproduced in this book. Any omissions will be rectified in subsequent printings if notice is given to the publishers.

Contents

Meet Harold the doctor

Harold

Have you ever been to see a doctor at a surgery?

Before work

Harold has his breakfast and reads the newspaper.

Harold drives to work.

Vrooommm

The day starts

Harold finds out about the patients who are waiting to see him.

Sue
the receptionist

He gets everything ready
for the first patient.

Leah isn't feeling very well.

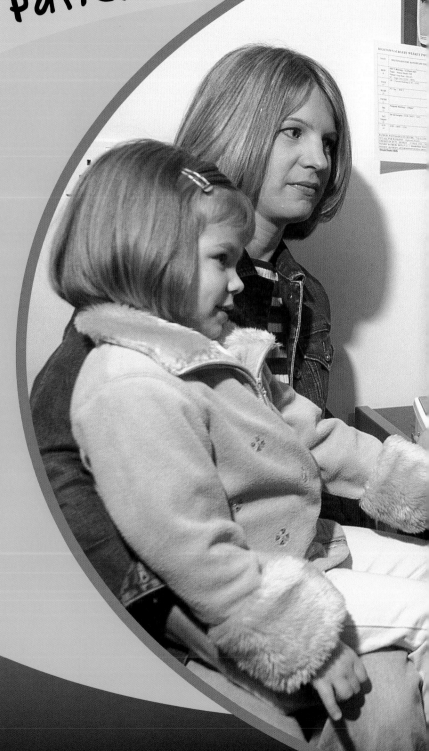

Do you go to see a doctor when you are ill?

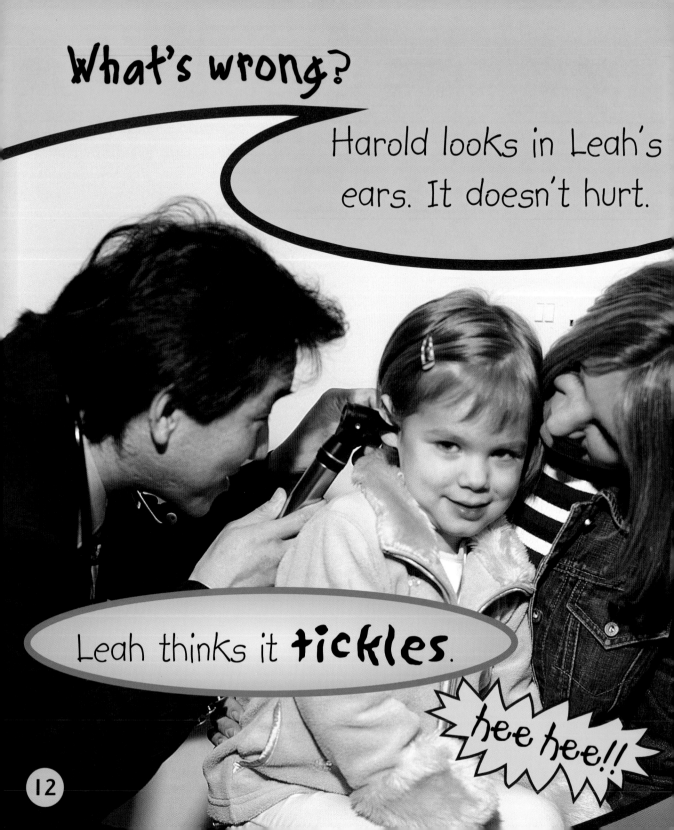

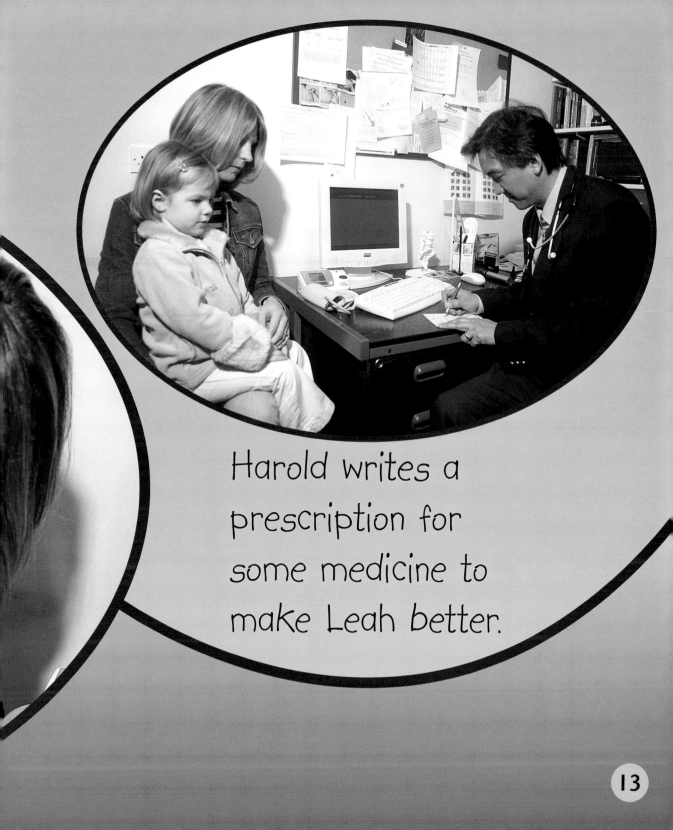

Harold writes a prescription for some medicine to make Leah better.

More patients

Harold takes a patient's blood pressure.

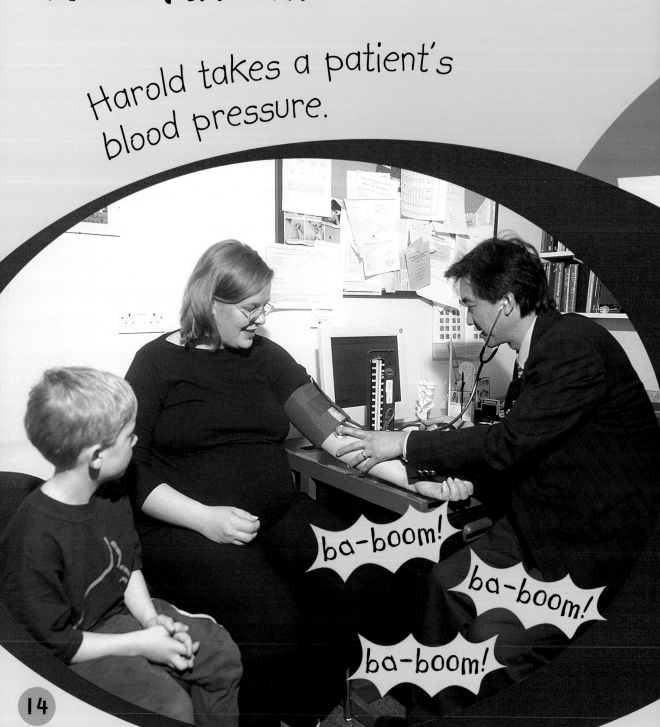

He gives a flu injection.

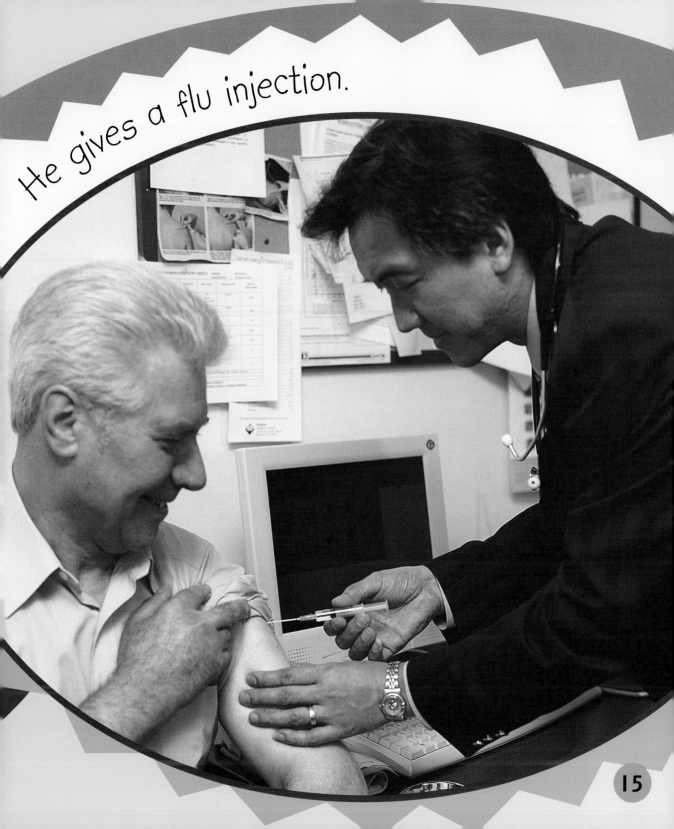

A break for lunch

Harold has telephone calls
to make and letters to write.

Baby clinic

Harold and Connie the health visitor get ready for the baby clinic.

Connie

Baby check-up

The baby is weighed.

Harold uses a stethoscope to listen to the baby's heart.

The day ends

Harold likes to relax and read the newspaper.

Snooze
the cat

Harold takes his pager with him when he goes to bed in case anyone needs him during the night.

Index

The end

Notes for adults

This series supports the young child's exploration of their learning environment and their knowledge and understanding of their world. The following Early Learning Goals are relevant to the series:
• Respond to significant experiences, showing a range of feelings when appropriate.
• Find out about events that they observe.
• Ask questions about why things happen and how things work.
• Find out about and identify the uses of everyday technology to support their learning.

The series shows the different jobs four professionals do and provides opportunities to compare and contrast them. The books show that like everyone else, including young children, they get up in the morning, go to bed at night, break for meals, and have families, pets and a life outside their work.

The books will help the child to extend their vocabulary, as they will hear new words. Some of the words that may be new to them in **A Day in the Life of a Doctor** are *surgery, receptionist, patient, prescription, medicine, blood pressure, injection, health visitor, clinic, stethoscope* and *pager*. Since words are used in context in the book this should enable the young child to gradually incorporate them into their own vocabulary.

The following additional information may be of interest:
The doctor wears his normal clothes when he sees patients so that he appears more approachable and informal. He examines ears with an auriscope and measures blood pressure with a sphygmomanometer. A health visitor is a nurse who has been especially trained to work with babies, young children and their families. Babies and young children are regularly seen by a doctor to check on their development.

Follow-up activities
The child could role play situations in a doctor's surgery. Areas could be set up to create a consulting room, a waiting room and a baby clinic. The child could also record what they have found out by drawing, painting or tape recording their experiences.